PRAISE FOR *VIEW FROM THE VOLCANO*

"Creating an industry—not just a business—at that time, when women were coming into their own…Kathy Clarke marshaled, cajoled and enlightened an entire industry. Her memoir offers encouragement for any young man or woman."

—Bob Schwager, Event Theme and Floral Designer

"A true pioneer in Hawai'i's hospitality industry, Kathy Clarke details her hilarious journey from tour desk to destination management company owner. She epitomizes the saying "If there's a will, there's a way." Fortunately no clients, suppliers, staff or family-members suffered bodily harm during her career, because orange is not her color. She is simply the best."

—Melissa DeLeon, President, MTI Events

PRAISE FOR *MY LIFE IS A ROAD ATLAS*

"Need a laugh? This set me on a circuitous route of a life with its uplifting and humorous episodes and outcomes. Easy to read in one sitting for a quick laugh and smile."

—Judy Folk, School Librarian, BA, MA, & MLIS

"If you've never met the author, by the time you're done with the book, you will WANT to meet her. This book is one that'll keep your attention. You will crack up laughing at the pace she kept and the guys she met. This is one amazing woman."

—Lani Olsen-Chong, Waimea Community Activist

Also by Kathy Clarke

My Life Is a Road Atlas

View from the Volcano
A REBEL'S CRUSADE IN
HAWAI'I TOURISM

———
THE HALI'A ALOHA SERIES
———

View from the Volcano

A REBEL'S CRUSADE IN HAWAI'I TOURISM

KATHY CLARKE

LEGACY ISLE
PUBLISHING

THE HALIʻA ALOHA SERIES
Darien Hsu Gee, Series Editor

Haliʻa Aloha ("cherished memories") by Legacy Isle Publishing is a guided memoir program developed in collaboration with series editor Darien Hsu Gee. The series celebrates moments big and small, harnessing the power of short forms to preserve the lived experiences of the storytellers. To become a Haliʻa Aloha author, please visit www.legacyislepublishing.net.

Legacy Isle Publishing is an imprint of Watermark Publishing, based in Honolulu, Hawaiʻi, and dedicated to "Telling Hawaiʻi's Stories" through memoirs, corporate biographies, family histories and other books.

© 2023 Katherine Pelca

All rights reserved. No part of this book may be reproduced in any form or by any electronic or mechanical means, including information retrieval systems, without prior written permission from the publisher, except for brief passages quoted in reviews.

Names in this book have been changed to protect the privacy of the individuals involved.

ISBN 978-1-948011-95-2 (print)
ISBN 978-1-948011-96-9 (ebook)

Legacy Isle Publishing
1000 Bishop St., Ste. 806
Honolulu, HI 96813
Telephone 1-808-587-7766
Toll-free 1-866-900-BOOK
www.legacyislepublishing.net

Printed in the United States

For all the amazing travel staff and industry suppliers
who supported me unconditionally, with aloha,
over the years.

You are the foundation of Hawai'i's travel industry.
Nothing happens without you!

Contents

I: Hawai'i Tourism is Born (1956–1980)
Wanted: Destination Travel Professional	6
Lahaina 1977	8
Life Before the Internet	11
The Oldest Profession	15
Earn While You Learn	17
Terry	19

II: Hawai'i Tourism and Me (1980–1989)
Maui No Ka Oi	25
What are the Dates?	29
On Being a Rebel	31
Anatomy of a Blue Cruise	34
Pineapple Princesses	36
Baby Bottle Toss	39
Lahaina 'Uhane	41
Inventing the Destination	44
Events Made Easy	47
I Cannot Resist a Mic	54

III: Hawai'i Tourism Evolves (1990–2008)
Random Firsts	60
The Sacrifice	65
IOU	67
Marketing Reinvented	68
Nothing is Impossible	72

The Great Waiomina	75
Herding Cats	78
Good Client Slips	80

IV: Inside Hawai'i Tourism (2009–2022)

Staff Meeting	85
Dear Client, Did You Read the Contract?	87
Experience and Wisdom	92
Hawai'i's Oldest Living DMC	95
Acknowledgments	100
Glossary	102

Apparently, I am an overachiever.

I

HAWAI'I TOURISM IS BORN
1956–1980

1956
Pioneer Mill & Amfac resolve to build Kā'anapali Resort. 150,000 tourists visit Hawai'i. Military spends over $350M in Hawai'i's economy. Construction is rampant.

1957-1958
Henry J. Kaiser builds geodesic dome at Hilton Hawaiian Village with friend Peter Fithian. Sheraton buys Royal Hawaiian, Moana Surfrider and Princess Ka'iulani in Waikīkī. TransPacific Airlines becomes Aloha Air. Barn owls imported from California.

1959
HAWAI'I STATEHOOD. Peter Fithian holds first Billfish Tournament in Kailua-Kona. Don Ho performs at Honey's Bar in Kāne'ohe—the audience sees a star.

1960
Tourism challenges sugar/pineapple industry in revenue. Military and construction are still major economic drivers. Hilo tsunami devastates the town's economy.

1961
Castle & Cooke purchases Dole Foods, controls the sleepy pineapple plantation island of Lāna'i. Elvis films *Blue Hawai'i* on Kaua'i.

1962-1964
Royal Lahaina, Maui Surf, Sheraton and Kā'anapali Beach hotels built on Maui. Lahaina's first three-day Whaling Spree inspires Helene Hale, Uncle George Na'ope and Gene Wilhelm to create the first Merrie Monarch festival in Hilo to boost economy.

1965
Royal Hawaiian Air begins flying Cessna 420s out of Kā'anapali Airstrip. "High School Harry" serves Bloody Marys at the Windsock Lounge.

1966-1967
I am a 16-year-old highway surfer girl in California. Endless Summer surf film released. Pleasant Hawaiian Holidays (PHH) contracts hotel rooms with Roy Kelley, Outrigger. Tourism hits the one million mark. Waikīkī is king.

1968-1969
I graduate from high school and live in Waikīkī for six months in 1969 and work at the International Market Place. Woodstock happens. Hippies find Hawai'i, live off the land and are regularly beat up by locals.

1970-1971
LK&P Railroad begins operation in Lahaina. Merrie Monarch Festival in Hilo adds hula competitions.

1970-1976
A free spirit, I travel around California and the western states trying on various lifestyles. See my first book, My Life is a Road Atlas, *for details.*

1970-1980
Major industries boom in Hawai'i: construction, military, tourism, sugar, pineapple. Maui is "found." Wholesale tour and travel is king.

1972
Patent for Rollaboard suitcase is granted.

1973
The island of Lāna'i begins transition from pineapple to resort. Maritz Travel opens Waikīkī office.

1974
40-year-old sugar laws expire causing sugar prices to fall. State of Hawai'i realizes tourism might be a cash cow.

1975
First personal desktop computers and videocassette recorders hit the market.

1976
Maui is first outer island to break one million visitors. Three million statewide.

1977
I arrive in Lahaina in February and sleep on my future husband's front porch. Kīlauea erupts.

1977-1979
I open my first tour desk at The Wharf and began operating groups at hotels. The incentive business is born. American Express (AMEX) begins ground operations for PHH. Texas International Airlines creates frequent-flyer program. Congress deregulates airlines in 1978. Hawaiian Air makes history with first all-female crew.

WANTED: DESTINATION TRAVEL PROFESSIONAL

Program and Event Manager:

Our product is *Service with Aloha!* Responsibilities include: preparing proposals, supplier purchase order coordination, client contact and ongoing communication. Applicant must be outgoing, sincere, friendly, fun, enjoy people, willing to take on responsibility, able to multitask on multilevels, all simultaneously. Must enjoy taking initiative, formulating and completing projects independently, conducting information research, be detail-oriented and able to handle multiple tasks under extreme pressure. The ideal candidate must have excellent written communication skills, be computer literate and proficient in Microsoft Word and Excel. Basic PowerPoint and Photoshop a plus. Must be willing to work days, nights, weekends and holidays. Minimum two years travel industry experience essential.

Pay commensurate with experience. Sliding commissions. Health benefits provided and you will most likely need them.

P.S. You must also possess the patience of a saint when your client proposes an unrealistic event expectation, especially at the last minute. Meticulously walk them through a "how this is going to look" scenario to steer them solidly in the right direction. You may be required to repeat the walk through, emphasizing potential disasters. The work entails exposure to jet fuel fumes and diesel bus exhausts. Days will be sprinkled with demanding clients, charming professionals, happy and grouchy attendees, and bus drivers who share unlimited aloha, as everyone pulls together to make everything work. You will experience euphoria when a new and creative event is completed successfully and be amazed as unpredictable, near-catastrophic situations unfold.

No additional compensation for stress or overtime, but you will be invited to wild parties (industry events and your clients'), build lasting friendships with suppliers, hotel partners and colleagues while enjoying a sense of immense pride and accomplishment at the end of a successful program. You will stay in Hawai'i's best ocean-view hotel rooms but leave at first light and return well after dark. You will have access to outstanding free food, plenty of alcohol and beautiful sunsets, but have no time for the pool. Apply to Kathy Clarke Hawai'i: Rock Solid Events and Destination Management Company with résumé and cover letter. We look forward to welcoming you to our team!

LAHAINA 1977

The first time I came to Hawai'i, in 1969, I was nineteen with $300 in my pocket and no return ticket. I lived in a studio apartment in Waikīkī on O'ahu at the corner of Kūhiō and Ka'iulani, and worked in the International Market Place selling pink and black coral jewelry from a cart owned by Don the Beachcomber. Six months later, out of money, I returned to California. For the next seven years I was a free spirit, traveling around California and the western states, trying on various lifestyles including hippie, biker chick and business manager. Ultimately, I decided the quality of men in California would never meet my expectations and the state was quickly going downhill. In February 1977, one month before my twenty-seventh birthday, I bought another one-way ticket and headed straight to Lahaina on Maui. I arrived without a place to stay, a job or a plan. This was normal for me.

The Kahului airport was small with an open-air rotunda; the branches of a huge tree reached up to the windy blue sky. On the tarmac side, high windows with supermarket-style glass doors were the only "gates."

The first few years, we bought booklets of airline tickets and tore a blank one off as we walked through the gate, occasionally filling in our name. I was very irritated when Aloha Airlines required us to stand in line for real tickets. Jeff Martin, my exasperated airline salesman, threatened to tattoo a bar code on my rump so I could walk straight through the gate.

Arriving passengers exited the tarmac directly into the circular driveway. Waiting mommies sat in their cars for hubbies arriving on the 5:45 p.m. flight from Oʻahu, their little children running forward, shouting, "Daddy! Daddy!" as they clutched their fathers' knees. The planes were 737s, flying interisland only. Aloha Airlines was king. Hawaiian Airlines had a terrible reservation system and grumpy counter people. That would all change.

Arriving at the Maui Airport in Kahului, I hopped a Grayline shuttle bus which dropped me at the Pioneer Inn in Lahaina. A room at the PI was beyond my means. Stowing my bags in their lobby, I headed to the harbor to find a connection for a place to stay. I ended up sleeping on the office porch of one of the charter boat companies. The owner stepped over me around midnight as he entered the office. (Three years later I married him.) I found a room to rent the next day.

In 1977, Lahaina was not the busy tourist town it is today. There was not one stoplight on the west side of the island, and Kāʻanapali Resort Hotels sported the only elevators. I bought a baby blue bicycle with fat tires and handlebar basket. On warm plumeriascented nights I pedaled home through dark side streets with a million stars overhead. The old pronunciation of the town's name, Lāhainā, means "cruel sun." You could always tell the locals from the visitors; when it rained, the locals ran out in the street, delighted.

Lahaina was still a wild whaling town in spirit. Sally Smyth rode her horse into Moki's Bar on Lahainaluna Road for a beer. Pioneer Inn also hosted a horse or two. Jim Bruce, founder of the first Hāna van tour company, held up the LK&P Railroad on horseback with a bevy of large travel agents on board (all travel agents were large in those days). Plied with enough Scotch, Jim would play his bagpipes. Rusty Nall, with his neatly trimmed red pirate beard, ran Windjammer Cruises and downed shots at the PI; his wife occasionally took him home in a shopping cart.

At the PI, Trevor Jones sang naughty Welsh sea shanties while Dave Paquette rocked out on jazz piano. Fleetwood Mac groupies in black pleather jackets, looking "goth" and dripping sweat in sweltering Lahaina, asked a local if they would get mobbed inside the PI. The kid laughed and said, "No, you're safe, everyone in there is more famous than you!" Kenny Loggins would have agreed. One night Elton John jammed at the Blue Max on Front Street. Nobody cared about celebrities—just an average night in Lahaina.

LIFE BEFORE THE INTERNET

Life was simple when I began my business in Lahaina in late 1977. My first computer was a Kaypro, which was basically a monitor mounted in a portable sewing machine case. See Wikipedia for pictures. It had floppy drives and no memory. My IBM Selectric typewriter and file folders were more practical. In the late seventies, there were no cell phones or fax machines. Telex, like copy machines, were expensive and complicated, and only used by large companies. Telephones were dial-up, no touch tone. Off island calls were expensive long distance. Answering machines were barely introduced and no one would leave a message on those damn things.

We placed calls from home, office or pay phones, sent invoices via US snail mail and shook hands on a deal. There were no Excel spreadsheets. Manifests and invoices were handwritten or typed. We collected attendees' tickets and called each airline to re-confirm reservations. We returned paper tickets as they boarded the departure bus, afraid they would be lost or packed in luggage.

People were not well traveled back then. Hawai'i tourism was predominantly FITs (Free Independent Travelers), booked by travel agents and wholesale tour companies fueled by Maritz Travel, Pleasant Hawaiian Holidays, Trade Wind Tours, Cartan Tours, Globus and E. F. McDonald. A cheap, one-week tour in Hawai'i visited four islands in seven days. O'ahu included a Society of Seven or Don Ho cocktail show, a Pearl Harbor tour and a scenic North Shore drive to Polynesian Cultural Center. Maui hosted a choice of snorkel sails or all-day sail to Lāna'i, a *lū'au* and a full-day tour of either Hāna or Haleakalā. The Island of Hawai'i included a tour of Volcanoes National Park and City of Refuge and a dinner cruise on Captain Beans' huge pontoon boat departing from Kailua-Kona pier. Kaua'i hosted a bus tour of Waimea Canyon (the Grand Canyon of the Pacific) and the Smith Family's flat-bottomed riverboat cruise up the Wailua River to the famous fern grotto where the Hawaiian Wedding Song echoed off the fern-covered walls.

Local tour guides traveled with the group, corralled luggage, wrangled buses, sold optional tours and pocketed huge tips. I knew many of the original tour escorts and employed several, long after they retired. George Ahuna and Moli Miller, with their sincere aloha, handled my O'ahu airports until they passed. In 2006, I secured a last-minute group of 1,400 attendees at the Hilton Hawaiian Village. Pono, Gary and Tani stepped up to handle the hospitality desk and transportation, saving my bacon. In 2014, after a desperate call from me, Ray T. agreed to manage transportation for over 2,400 convention attendees and 900 VIPs staying at multiple Waikīkī hotels. There is no way I could have done it without him. Brenda Lee, one of my favorites, was so tiny my daughter called her "Smalls" which amused Brenda greatly. These folks were there from the beginning and the industry was built on their genuine aloha.

In the early 1980s, incentive programs were on the horizon. Maritz (originally selling watches as retirement rewards), created "premium books," rewarding top salespeople in any industry with a toaster or a refrigerator selected from the book. It was the same concept as the Green Stamps and Gold Bond stamps that the grocery store gave out. Maritz added an all-expenses-paid big-city weekend getaway for two with hotel, dinner and a show. It was so popular that companies started giving top winners travel incentives to more exotic destinations, then increased to larger groups to manage costs. Built on the wholesale tour and travel model, companies upgraded all components and soon a trip to Hawai'i was the ultimate reward for reaching a sales goal. A percentage allocated for the travel reward cost was built into the goal and "incentive travel" was born.

When preparing for a program, I called the activity supplier, gave them the date, time, inclusions and passenger count. We loaded the attendees on a bus and told the driver where to deliver them. The drivers, miraculously, always found the right place. The boat crew kept an eye out, met them at the bus and reloaded the returns on any bus standing by. Ninety-five percent of the time it was the right bus. There was no advance staff confirming readiness, timing, cleanliness or facilitating returns, yet somehow attendees left the hotel and got back. Everyone pitched in, shared aloha, and loved their work. Hula dancers hugged attendees as they departed. Expectations were met with genuine aloha and there were no hyperactive meeting planners micromanaging everything. It was just me, the client, the attendees and wonderful industry partners, sharing aloha.

I figured it out as I went along, inventing procedures and forms, innovating as needed and operating programs with no credentials whatsoever. I had no idea something might be considered impossible by others. I just did it anyway.

After a program, the tour suppliers sent an invoice, I sent the client a bill and we all got paid. That was it. In the late eighties, mainland clients went "corporate." They wanted proposals, letters of agreement, contracts and even, heaven forbid, insurance!

The state airports division recognized a cash cow. They required greeter permits and proof of insurance for the privilege of setting foot on airport grounds. This gave them a means to charge greeters and transportation companies a 3 percent fee on arrival costs. The boat operations paid 3 percent of their gross income to the Harbors Division. Hawai'i state pyramid-taxing at its finest! I want a scam like that!

THE OLDEST PROFESSION

As a mainland *haole* transplanted to Lahaina, I thought slinging mai tais on a dinner cruise or selling tours from a faux tiki hut on Front Street was Hawai'i tourism.

My first activity desk was a small triangle set back from the sidewalk across from the famous banyan tree fronting the newly built Wharf Shopping Center. In 1977, a tour desk on Front Street was an honorable profession: no time shares, no hawkers, no obnoxious gimmicks to attract attention. The only other activity desk, owned by Tom Barefoot, was kitty-corner, backed by the Pioneer Inn and an ice cream parlor. Tom had enjoyed a monopoly and was not happy when my not-yet-husband built my plexiglass brochure racks and storage space. Occasionally, I would call Tom from my canvas-shaded perch and ask how he was doing. From across the street, he would look up, scowl at me and hang up the phone. Phone manners notwithstanding, Tom was an excellent businessman. When his landlord replaced his prime location with a multi-parrot photo op, he moved down the street and developed one of the first online tour websites.

My very lucrative activity sales business ended when the shopping center manager suggested he would extend my one-year lease if I slept with him. I declined. Tom Roach, founder of the Royal Lahaina Lūʻau, apologized profusely for outbidding me but I suspect he didn't have to sleep with anyone!

During this time, hotel concierges seldom booked tours. They made restaurant reservations, assisted with special requests and reconfirmed airline tickets. The hotel sales staff shared my name with small meeting groups and conferences (both notorious for nonexistent budgets) to assist with activity bookings. For free, I would don my fresh flower *lei* and *muʻumuʻu* and place my brochure assortment and vouchers in a straw tote along with my dark blue Bank of Hawaiʻi zippered money pouch. Away I went, selling tours and pocketing my commissions, becoming a reliable resource and valuable perk for the hotels. Cash, check or traveler's checks only. The mainland conference planners thought I was a gift from heaven.

A year later, I wandered down Front Street and found Higgins Madigan, the property manager for the Lahaina Marketplace. He promptly gave me a small four-by-four booth right across from the seawall. Front Street now hosted three activity desks. My time at the Marketplace lasted until I presented Higgins with an idea for a new and better booth, modeled after the ʻIolani Palace Bandstand. He liked it so much, he found someone else to build it and booted me out, without even a courtesy offer for a sleepover.

EARN WHILE YOU LEARN

In 1982, while enjoying my panoramic view of Lahaina Roadstead, Lānaʻi and stunning sunsets from my activity booth, I was approached by a gentleman who had booked a large incentive group at the newly built Hyatt Kāʻanapali. He contracted me to arrange the hosted group tours in December and coordinate transportation during the program. Of course, I said yes.

Incentive groups were still a new concept at that time and twelve hundred attendees were by far the largest group I had ever operated. I had no real clue, but I created spreadsheets, activity boarding passes and mechanisms for each guest to sign up for tours on site. Many of those exact forms still pop up in the hands of present-day travel staff.

When my client arranged a site inspection in November, I was seven months pregnant—a fact I had failed to mention sooner. At thirty days out, despite possible concerns, his only choice was to continue our agreement. There was not enough staff to manage the restaurants and bus stops for multiple complicated international divisions dining in Lahaina, Kāʻanapali and Kapalua. At eight months pregnant, big as a house, ankles swollen like ski boots, I dispatched three bus routes for two dine-around nights from the back door of the Hyatt. *By myself.*

Events and entertainment were out of my league, but I was comfortable with group tour arrangements, and I had an artist's conception of how the airport transfers would work. The arrivals went well and loading bodies onto hotel departure buses, at the correct time, was easy. Sending their luggage ahead, not so much.

In theory, the bags arrived at the airport, went through agriculture inspection, then were tagged with pre-printed airline bag tags from manifests sent early. As guests arrived, they identified their luggage and proceeded to the check-in counter to surrender their bags. Smaller groups of fifty attendees and a hundred bags were easy. Twenty-four hundred bags, were another story. We packed the morning trucks as tight as possible, loosely in chronological order by flight departure time. All luggage destined for afternoon and evening flights were sent later. Oops. An excessive bag disaster in the making.

At that time, the lava rock wall at the end of the Maui airport extend over one hundred feet in front of baggage claim. We covered its length with bags four feet high. Guests had to find their bag in the mass grave of unorganized luggage. I am not exactly sure why my staff or the porters let me live, but being professionals, they got through it. My client, no more sophisticated than I was, just shook his head. I'm happy to say my future airport departure procedures were impeccable.

TERRY

In 1979, between Front Street activity desks and free hotel hospitality desks, Terry Yawata came into my life. I am sure he would have told anyone who asked that he found me on a street corner, which was technically true, due to my sidewalk activity-desk locations.

Well-connected in the Hawai'i tour and meeting industry, Terry was a natural conduit, connecting people, advancing agendas and facilitating industry growth. He was deeply immersed in the O'ahu travel industry, recognized opportunities and always put them to good use.

Around 1981, Terry was promoted by Maritz Travel to manage their entire Hawai'i operation. This was a very big deal for young Mr. Yawata and launched him on his successful career. At seven months pregnant with my first child, my husband and I were invited to his congratulatory reception at the Kāhala Hotel on O'ahu. Sipping orange juice from a champagne glass, my obvious belly looked overly large as I stood in a circle of Maritz's top VIPs from St. Louis. At that time, Midwestern businessmen were extremely conservative and proper. They still wore dress shirts in Hawai'i, not an aloha shirt or khaki pant in sight.

As Terry introduced me to his new bosses, I turned to him, tilted my head and asked coyly, "Terry, now that you have your big promotion, are you going to marry me?" The shocked silence around the group was deafening. I think it was the only time I saw Terry speechless. He took a step back, mumbled something and then laughed. The stuffed shirts concluded it was a jest and abruptly changed the subject in case it wasn't.

Terry was raised in traditional Japanese style. He was short, slightly round, with tiny eyes and a receding hairline. He was intensely private, loved golf, adored blondes and welcomed every challenge. He took loving care of his parents until they passed.

Occasionally, Terry would show up unannounced at our house in Lahaina. He was appalled if I didn't have a cold beer handy. He always enjoyed my babies from a distance and told us how lucky we were. I suspected he missed not having a family of his own. He made suggestions that furthered my career or his agenda, offered insider tips on industry opportunities, opened doors and then shoved me through.

In the early days, he contracted me to bring my staff of activity desk ladies to the hotel and set up an on-site tour desk for his large groups. His company handled the hotels, events and airport transfers. My "Ladies of Aloha" lined up with dial-out house phones, brochures, vouchers and pre-compiled lists of the week's available tours. We sold thousands of dollars in tours, booked restaurants, handed out departure notices and found lost sunglasses. Terry paid a stipend for our presence, and I kept all the tour commissions. Win-win.

In the mid-nineties, I hosted an event for a group of meeting planners at Parker Ranch's Puʻu Opelu venue on the Big Island. It was a beautifully catered event, with elegant linen, tropical florals and Hawaiian music. I brought my teenage daughter and one of her hula sisters to perform for our guests. They enticed Kalani Nakoa, one of our hotel partners, to join them in a lively, slightly naughty performance of the hula "ʻA ʻOia," about a man winning over his new love.

At the end of the evening, Terry smiled at me. "I am officially impressed," he said. "You have finally arrived." High praise from my good friend of many years.

Around 2017, he was consulting for one of my competitors, and over coffee he suggested he could help my company grow also. I had built my business over thirty-five years, raised a family and was well known in the industry. I laughed out loud. "Terry, exactly why would I want to grow? I 'arrived' a long time ago!" He paused, considering, gave me one of his special, thoughtful smiles and responded, "You may be right!"

Terry was my first real exposure to the destination management side of the industry and in many ways was my mentor, as he was for so many other people. Terry never met a stranger, he welcomed everyone.

His circle of friends, associates and significant industry influence spanned fifty years. During that time he touched so many lives.

In 2018, he was diagnosed with cancer. He told no one and a few months later, left us quietly on December 7, 2018. I flew to Oʻahu for his funeral. The hall was packed with industry people who all sat in the back of the room. His family sat up front and spoke. We began to realize that they had no idea who Terry really was. He was a beloved nephew or cousin to them but to the rest of us, he was an industry icon, an esteemed friend and would be deeply missed.

II

HAWAI'I TOURISM AND ME
1980–1989

1980

I invite my future husband to our wedding and wait to see if he shows up. Open my second activity desk in front of Lahaina Marketplace.

1981

My first birth child, Cinnamon, makes her appearance. Hurricane 'Iwa devastates Kaua'i.

1982

I operate 1,200 pax group eight months pregnant at Hyatt Kā'anapali in December. American Express Travel is founded. Over half of sugar plantations are shut down. Hawai'i Island agriculture begins transition to mac nuts and coffee. Pakalōlō is Maui's #1 ag product.

1983

My second birth child, Kawehi, is born. I purchase my Buick Riviera convertible. Throw a baby bottle at two policemen. My stepson, Adam, visits for the summer and never goes back to his mom's house. Children's birth order number officially changes with Adam as number one. Travel agents enter the online tech marketing trend with America One. Frequent Flyer program begins as Travel Plus Worldwide. Kīlauea erupts; starts destructive flow to the sea.

1984

Last sugar plantations close. Mauna Loa erupts. Stouffers Wailea opens.

1985

Nurse newborn third birth child (now child number four), Kaleo, at Hyatt Maui during 450 pax group in April. My business continues to grow. David Murdock purchases island of Lāna'i. AMEX and PHH terminate their joint operation. Maritz peaks then dwindles due to internal strife.

1987

My fourth birth child, Cayenne (child number five), is born. My husband's Lahaina boat business folds. Transient Accommodations Tax (TAT) goes into effect.

1988

Move to Waimea, Big Island, with four children under seven years old. With no incentive business on Hawai'i Island. I cashier at supermarket to pay bills. Hired at Royal Waikoloa (Marriott) in the executive office. Hyatt Waikoloa (now Hilton) and Ritz Carlton Mauna Lani (now Fairmont Orchid) open. Hawai'i Convention Center opens on O'ahu.

1989

I win a contract for 1,200 pax group six weeks out. First big program for the Hyatt Waikoloa. Establishes the foundation for my Big Island career. Japanese bubble bursts, real estate plunges. Berlin Wall falls. Tiananmen Square massacre. Airlines begin "codeshares."

MAUI NO KA OI

I did my best to start a rebellion in the visitor industry on Maui. (Yes, John M., I have been a rebel for a *very* long time.) The Kāʻanapali Beach Operators Association (KBOA) was originally formed in the early 1980s as a marketing arm to promote Kāʻanapali Resort, as the Hawaiʻi Visitors Bureau (HVB) was Oʻahu-centric and outer islands were treated like the red-headed stepsister. HVB told Maui to pay their dues and keep quiet while Oʻahu used funds at their discretion to market Waikīkī. Kāʻanapali Resort took marketing into their own hands, but ultimately needing more funds, they reached out to westside restaurants, tour and activity operators, soliciting their membership dollars for entry into the elite hotel executive club.

Boat and van tours were always the soldiers left dying on the battlefield while the hotel operators crusaded over their languishing bodies, marketing the resort's ocean-view rooms, stunning white-sand beaches, lush golf courses, fine dining and nothing else. They were convinced that visitors came to Maui for hotel rooms and golf clubs. KBOA felt tour and restaurant operators should be grateful their marketing brought visitors to Maui's shores so the suppliers could profit from KBOA's efforts. It never occurred to them that the wide variety of boat, van, helicopter tours, lūʻau and local Hawaiian culture might provide additional incentive to visit Maui. They didn't ask for marketing input, tour write-ups or a single brochure. The membership dues only sold hotel rooms.

The token supplier members were, however, invited to attend the annual meeting as a modest display of inclusiveness. I didn't intend to ruffle feathers, but I was young, with little tact and no idea of how all the pieces fit together. I wanted to ask what they were doing with our dues, maybe see a financial statement and point out that we received no direct benefit from our membership dues and inquire how we could improve the relationship!

I arrived at the annual meeting ready to voice my concerns and rally support for the little guys. Two very large hotel execs seated themselves on either side of me. My husband, Chuck, seeing me flanked by such impressive deterrents and knowing that I planned to speak up, chose a seat several rows away.

When the moment came, my escorts leaned toward me but before I could stand up, Chuck took the floor and, to my surprise, delivered my speech. As it turned out, it was more effective coming from him than feisty little female me. The KBOA board was flustered, fellow tour operators chimed in, and the Good Ol' Boys ultimately acquiesced to tour operators' involvement in marketing, however limited.

Maui, an "outer island," had little connection to O'ahu. Enter Frank Blackwell, an icon who put Maui on the map. He partnered with the Maui chapter of the Visitors Bureau (MVB) and hit the road, traveling across the United States and attending every *TravelAge West*, travel agent and general travel expo in existence. To support his marketing expenses, MVB went to the county council and solicited dedicated funds.

O'ahu got wind of the generous dollar allotment and informed MVB that, as an extension of the HVB, they must give the money to them and they would parcel it back as they saw fit. No. Just no. MVB promptly seceded from the union and kept the cash. They formed an independent nonprofit, disassociated themselves from the HVB and suggested they go back to O'ahu. It was an unprecedented historic moment.

Frank was a road warrior who knew that tourists did not come to Hawai'i for a hotel room and invited the tour operators to join him on the road. Soon "Maui Nō Ka 'Oi" was born as Lahaina's top tour operators shared aloha in ever widening circles. Don Martin, from Holo Holo Tours, attended with his huge Hawaiian *lauhala* hat and contagious bombastic laugh. His bright aloha shirts did not hide his big *ōpū* and his constantly open arms welcomed everyone with true aloha and kindness. Jim Bruce, tour founder, wore slightly smaller hats and aloha shirts over a more modest ōpū as he refilled bowl after bowl with the original Kitch'n Cook'd Maui Potato Chips. Chocolate and salted mac nuts disappeared into travel agent totes as the dapper Rusty Nall from Windjammer Cruises flouted his gold braided captain's cap and white shirt with black and gold epaulets. Tom Roach, founder of the original Royal Lahaina Lūʻau, handed out lei and occasionally brought a hula dancer along to perform in the Hawaiʻi booths. Chuck Clarke from Vida Mia-Viajero Cruises wore his New England fisherman's cap and charmed the ladies with his Robert Kennedy look-alike smile. The LK&P Railroad sent Dan Ranger with his souvenir giveaways and *kolohe* spirit.

These six men were Frank's secret weapon. No travel agent or would-be visitor could resist their combined Spirit of Aloha and invitations to visit Maui Nō Ka ʻOi! They set the bar for aloha on the road and Maui surpassed Oʻahu, taking over the Hawaiʻi travel industry marketing. I often thought of these men as pirates, sailing from one trade show to the next. Their capers on the road were legendary and worthy of a much lengthier future tale.

WHAT ARE THE DATES?

I had six babies over ten years and raised my stepson while building my business on Maui and Hawai'i Island. My office was always at home, no matter how many employees I had. After the fourth child, I hired live-in nannies. People always asked how I did it. The answer was always the same. *I have no idea.* Truly.

In early 1985, I contracted a group of four hundred and fifty attendees for the end of April at the Hyatt Kā'anapali. It was the usual format; airport transfers, choice of hosted tours, dine arounds. When my client came for the site inspection, I was seven months pregnant—again. I told him we were fine, as I was due the first part of April. My son was two weeks late; I had the doctor induce labor so I would have time to finish the program prep.

Kaleo, at two weeks old, was the perfect baby. My husband cared for him and when Kaleo was hungry (every four hours on the dot), his father brought him to the hotel and waited until I was available. I would take little Kaleo in a back room, nurse his sweet little self, hand him over and go back to work.

During my ten child birthing years, my clients would call and ask if I would be pregnant during their program. My first question was always, "What are the program dates?"

ON BEING A REBEL

A good revolution has no beginning or end. It comes out of thin air when no one is looking. *Bam! Revolution! Change We Must! Question Authority! Stop the War!* Little precursors of pointed quips, uttered by instigators until a clarion call goes out and people gather with like-minded rebels to support their mutual passion. I love being a rebel!

I had been out of the convention circuit for two years, giving birth to kid number three or four, when I attended my first mainland trade show in a while. I was appalled that the setup didn't remotely look like a Hawai'i destination booth. Aloha shirts were in scarce supply. The Hawai'i Visitor Bureau marketing folks had turned our formerly spacious and welcoming destination culture into rows of ten-by-ten pipe and drape booths with black-and-white signage, tan table skirting, the occasional tropical print runner and glossy color posters on collapsible wire banner frames. It was not the Hawaiian marketing brand I had come to expect.

Being the reserved, diplomatic person that I am, I cornered the Bureau's resident honchos to remind them of outstanding past Hawaiian marketing events. I finished with "What the hell happened to aloha?!" (They still hate to see me coming.) Evidently, I made my point. At the next trade show planning meeting, a new design concept was presented by Pris Texeira, HVB's new marketing director. A prototype design featured individual bamboo booths with thatching, tropical florals and Hawaiian prints, all strategically placed in our open-air destination space with stunning graphics. Aloha attire would henceforth be mandatory. Aloha was back! I was invited to join the planning committee, most likely to circumvent future tirades.

One of our state legislators had targeted HVB. She visited the industry's biggest trade show in Chicago looking for wasted money. Obviously, she had never encountered Chicago trade unions who charged a four-hour minimum for a plumber to bring a bucket of water for the florals! I didn't like her bulldog attack on our industry. In our short meeting I affirmed the bureau's strong member support and the Chicago trade show's importance to the industry. I suggested any alleged money problems stemmed from the legislature and not HVB.

In 1987, the legislature implemented a Transient Accommodations Tax (TAT) to increase state revenue, fund a convention center in Honolulu, and further threaten the golden goose. A portion of the tax was allocated to each county to offset the impact of visitors on county infrastructure.

In 1998 the legislature created the Hawai'i Tourism Authority (HTA), an additional level of bureaucracy intended to "direct" tourism, provide oversight and integrate cultural, community and natural resources. More specifically, it would oversee the new convention center and HVB, which had operated autonomously with little accountability for years. The legislature, through HTA, was able to micromanage Hawai'i's lucrative travel industry.

Over time, the TAT rate increased but the statutory allocation distributed to the counties was slowly reduced to a fraction of total collections. Effective in January 2022, the greedy state decided to keep *all* TAT revenue, regardless of the island generating it, and told the counties to add their own county accommodations tax to make up the shortfall. Hotel contracts and client operating budgets had been approved and finalized months prior. All incentive programs and FIT visitors were now 3 percent over budget.

Small businesses paid the price for this budget shortfall. Clients cut out florals and linens, reduced or eliminated entertainment, canceled tours and anything else that was expendable, hurting desperate small businesses just coming off COVID-19 shutdowns. I have no patience. As Forrest Gump said, "Stupid is as stupid does."

ANATOMY OF A BLUE CRUISE

A blue cruise does not mean a "sad" sail, though it can be, admittedly, a little "off color."

When I was pregnant with my fourth child in 1987, my two best friends decided a "ladies only" cruise with male strippers was a great idea. I provided the catamaran, at a reduced rate. They found the strippers, sold tickets, supplied veggie crudités and cheap wine. They placed a newspaper ad for male candidates, screened out the perverts and held auditions in the garage. The lack of natural talent on Maui quickly became apparent. My entrepreneurial friends measured and made costumes, diligently choreographed musical stripping routines and role-played ways to make ladies feel special and pampered.

On cruise night the attending ladies dressed to the nines. The gentlemen greeted them with grace, kissing hands and looking directly into their eyes. Wearing tight, low-cut jeans, bow-tie collars and cuffs, the charming hosts mingled with the ladies. As scheduled, each host discreetly disappeared, changed costumes and returned for their performance.

The gentlemen had learned their lessons well. The ladies went wild, and many dollar bills went into G-strings or similar.

But it was Captain Rafael who outperformed, grabbing an overhead bar and wrapping his legs around the shoulders of a laughing, squealing young lady in the front row. Steve, aka Tarzan, swung into view next. He was a natural. He loved his work and later built a career on baby showers, birthdays and bachelorette parties.

The next cruise sold out in three days. The Maui liquor commission placed a female observer on board, allegedly to monitor protocol and intoxication levels. The ladies were not disappointed with the refined performances. One stripper eventually married a lovely attendee. "How I Met Your Mother" comes to mind.

We decided an obviously pregnant lady might be a killjoy on the cruise, so I stayed on the pier full of husbands and boyfriends waiting for the boat's return. I asked one guy if he was okay with his lady going on a male stripper cruise. He laughed and said, "Absolutely! The best sex I ever had was after the last one!" Well, there you are. Happy to be of service.

PINEAPPLE PRINCESSES

In 1986, my best friend decided we should start a business. She grew up working in her father's hardware store and she managed the first van tour business on Maui. I had managed my husband's tour boat business "from behind" for almost eight years, while growing my destination management business and, oh yeah, having babies.

My friend was bored, unemployed and ready for a change. We each kicked in $5,000 and The Lānaʻi Pineapple Place was born, and we began selling "Take Home Pineapples" in brightly printed boxes for visitors flying home. We negotiated with the Lānaʻi plantation manager to buy cases of pineapples direct from the island, secured our agricultural inspection permit, ordered printed boxes from Weyerhaeuser on Oʻahu and found retail space outdoors, tucked under the stairs of my alma mater, the Wharf Shopping Center.

Boat crews loaded pines on the day-tour boats traveling between Maui and Lānaʻi. Dressed in tank tops and short-shorts, we unloaded forty-five-pound cases of pineapples, stacked them five high on the back of my partner's 1974 red Jeep Wrangler and headed to her garage. As business grew, we rented warehouse space in Lahaina's only light industrial area, built a walk-in refrigerator and added a cargo van. My persistent partner scared the heck out of Mr. Oredomo, the original Maui sweet onion farmer, until he agreed to sell us his famous onions just to make her go away.

We started selling sweet Lāna'i pines to local restaurants when take-home sales were slow. Kitchen managers could not resist our winning smiles and our small, sweet pines that made perfect pineapple boats and mai tai garnish. The restaurant deliveries boomed. Our petite delivery girl, dressed in tank top and shorts, could swing a fifty-pound case of pines over her head. Little did we know she was dealing drugs along her route but, hey, the kitchen managers loved her.

We were carrying three hundred cases per week on our midnight Lāna'i runs when a major hotel called in an order. That tipped the scales. On O'ahu, Fred's Wholesale Produce noticed they weren't selling many pines on the west side of Maui. Lāna'i regularly shipped containers of pines to Fred's where they were dispersed to the various island markets. Suddenly, we were competitors to big business.

At Fred's "request," Dole Pineapple, owned by Castle & Cooke, stopped selling to us. We flew to O'ahu and confronted the big cheese, who unapologetically said, "Sorry, no can." Mysteriously, Weyerhaeuser refused to sell us any more boxes. The hotel and several restaurants said they could not buy from us anymore or Fred's would not deliver their other produce.

The local newspaper did an article on our David and Goliath challenge. Initially helpful, Goro Hokama, the Lānaʻi County councilman would no longer return our calls. Our retail lease was coming up, I was six months pregnant again and there was no one to sleep with. The Pineapple Princesses had been downgraded to the Pupule Princesses.

BABY BOTTLE TOSS

In the eighties, my husband owned and operated Seabird Cruises in Lahaina. In addition to the all-day sail to Lānaʻi, we had created an all-day sail to Molokaʻi, anchoring in a protected cove on the east end. Guests swam ashore for a beautiful beach day and an authentic Hawaiian lūʻau catered by Pearl and Sonny Punahele. We had reclaimed taro patches, cleared overgrown land and built restrooms at the back of the property.

True to form, my husband delayed getting the bathroom building permits and, once approved, neglected to sign the final permit. On a sleepy Sunday morning in Lahaina, two police officers appeared at my door to arrest Chuck on a bench warrant, issued by a judge who expected a timely signature. I had a six-month-old on my hip and a baby bottle in my hand when I answered the door. With postpartum hormones rampaging, I was less than pleased with the reason for their visit. I went ballistic and proceeded to cuss those poor guys out, ranting, raving and throwing the baby bottle at them, fortunately with very bad aim. They were very patient and understanding, apologized for the arrest and transported Chuck to the police station, advising me I could bail him out with $200 cash in about an hour.

I said that would be a cold day in hell. I considered my limited options as I fed lunch to my two little ones, loaded them in the car and dragged both babies inside the police station. I was furious with the children's father for weeks but very glad "assaulting a policeman with a baby bottle" was not a thing.

LAHAINA ʻUHANE

Built over an ancient stream bed, my Lahaina office on Waineʻe Street, was haunted. The house was on the edge of the Lahaina Historical District, which began on the west side of Waineʻe Street and extend to the ocean. The Old Lahaina Prison, directly across the street, incarcerated drunken sailors in the late 1800s. David Malo, author of the renowned book *Hawaiian Antiquities* (considered a classic source for ancient Hawaiian culture), had lived in the house on the corner. Queen Keōpūolani, by virtue of bloodlines the highest-ranking royalty in all Hawaiʻi, wife of Kamehameha I and mother of Kamehameha II and III, was buried a block away at Waiola Church. The historical walking tours of Lahaina focused on Waineʻe and Front Streets. There was a lot of history on that little street.

A small building, just off the back door, held an *ofuro* (Japanese soaking tub) and a Japanese pear tree grew nearby. The house was previously home to a Chinese couple who raised the children of a wealthy Japanese businessman. Waineʻe means "moving water," and there was a small sinkhole in the back yard, probably due to the old stream bed. I kept filling it with dirt; years later, our renters made it into a sunken BBQ pit.

In 2002 I remodeled the house, turning two bedrooms into staff offices. I stayed in the master bedroom while on island. Dreams were always vivid at this house, and one night I was sure there was someone in my bed. I had a perfect sense of him, laying with his back to me, smooth round shoulders, a balding head, not tall, quietly snoring. His spiritual presence was real, but I was never afraid as I drifted in a half-dream state wondering how this could be. Later I decided it was the old Chinese man who had lived there. This half-dream state became a regular occurrence.

Then one night, again in a half sleep, I heard someone knock on the back door and call out. My spirit self got up and went to the door which had a large window in the upper half. I saw a young Hawaiian man in a white shirt with a shaved head. A young boy with a pensive look stood next to him. I was not afraid.

"Can we come in?" he asked.

I was mildly surprised but said, "No, I am sorry, I cannot let you in." His face become distressed, and he repeated the request. Again, I said, "No, I cannot." The boy looked worried.

"Please let us in. If you don't, he cannot pass." The man gestured to the boy, and I saw fear in the boy's face as his shoulders slumped and he looked down. The man was not angry, but he was dispirited, and his face was sad.

I repeated, "I'm sorry, but I cannot let you in."

He turned, hopeless, and they disappeared. I was sorrowful but also felt I had no other choice. My spirit self went back to bed and to sleep.

I later asked Vince, a trusted Hawaiian friend, if I had made the right choice. He said yes, as you don't know who or what you are letting in. I still wonder if I made the right decision and will always regret the look on the boy's face.

INVENTING THE DESTINATION

Our move from Maui to Waimea in 1988 was motivated by Lahaina's terrible public schools and my oldest child's acceptance at Hawai'i Preparatory Academy (HPA). My husband had lost his Lahaina boat business, his mid-life crisis was in full swing, and Waimea seemed like a good idea.

The Big Island had no incentive business yet. The Mauna Lani Bay and Mauna Kea Beach Hotels favored wealthy repeat families and independent travelers but frowned on groups. The Sheraton (now the Marriott) was a wholesale tour and travel hotel. Kona hotels were strictly budget properties. The Hyatt Waikoloa (now Hilton) and the Ritz Carlton Mauna Lani (now Fairmont) were still under construction. The Hāpuna Prince and Four Seasons were barely on the radar.

So, there I was, with four children under seven and ready to work, but unable to do what I did best. The Big Island had no idea what an incentive program was! My Maui business was shrinking as I was no longer visible, and I needed employment.

I took a job as a cashier at Sure Save Super Market nights and weekends and a temp agency placed me at the Royal Waikoloan (now Marriott) maintaining the "event space book" in the executive office. Right up my alley! In six weeks, I learned the job, wrote a job description and trained my replacement. I stayed on at the hotel and worked in various departments with Gordon Hentschel, the GM; Pris Texeira, Director of Sales; Roy Cordiero, Sales Manager; and Peter Thoene in Convention Services. Doreen DeSilva, then a catering admin, is now the HR director at the Fairmont Orchid.

In June 1989, a repeat client called with a group of twelve hundred attendees on the Big Island. I told him the island suppliers' lack of incentive training would be challenging but I could do it.

Having worked with me before, he asked, "Are you pregnant?"

"Not right now. When's the program?"

"In six weeks," he said.

"Six weeks out? Twelve hundred attendees?" I had not operated a program on this island, had no resources and little local knowledge, but "impossible" never occurred to me. "No problem," I said. "At least we know for sure I won't be pregnant. Which hotel?"

The Hyatt had been open less than a year with only one group of four hundred guests previously. When I first began in Maui there was no incentive business, so "training up" the Big Island was not intimidating. Been there, done that! I found "Square" Kalima at Grayline Tours in Kona and I am sure he thought I was the dumbest reverse coconut to ever fall from a tree. I pulled every bit of local knowledge out of his kind, but slightly exasperated, brain. He filled in all the "local knowledge" blanks, and I will forever be grateful.

I identified tour suppliers from *This Week* magazine. The group's VIP requested a private sailboat with a well-stocked bar at his disposal twenty-four-seven. I found a beautiful wooden sailboat and asked Capt. Bob Hogan, the owner, for a daily rate. He gave me a number and I said, "No." He started to hedge but I stopped him.

"Bob, that is not enough. *For you.* You need to charge more."

In training mode, I gave him an amount five times his proposal. The VIP went sailing once during the five-day charter and Capt. Bob kept a very extensive, top-shelf bar. I built my Big Island reputation on this group and began operating on both Maui and Hawai'i Island.

EVENTS MADE EASY

I had no formal training in the event industry. I attended many special events trade shows, wrote up descriptions of theme events I had no idea how to source or produce and spent a fair amount of time perusing prom night catalogs for ideas.

In the 1980s there were no event production companies in Hawai'i. O'ahu had stage and lighting companies, party equipment and tent rentals but the outer islands had nothing until Envisions Entertainment was founded on Maui in 1995. Hotels carried a variety of linen and used their in-house florists. Storyboards (a visual "artist's conception" of event components), a load-in-out schedule and event timelines were unknown. DMCs (destination management companies) and hotels realized events made money, and elaborate theme events took on a life of their own.

I learned how to do events from my children. There was no occasion too trivial that could not be turned into a full-fledged extravaganza. It started with birthday parties. The Big Island had no resources, so raising six young kids required innovation. The Fun

Express novelties catalogue was my inspiration for a variety of themes presented to the current birthday child and, later, clients.

Kekai had an Ugly Bug Ball with plastic spiders and creepy crawlers scattered on the tables and mixed in the candy bowls and a face painter who transformed little faces into exotic creatures and insects. Both girls and boys attended Cayenne's party as no gender walls had been built yet. With a pile of cheap straw cowboy hats, silk flowers, feathers, random ribbon lengths and a glue gun, the kids decorated outlandish hats they happily took home.

Occasionally, the birthday was a simple cake and ice cream event. I didn't understand the word "simple." For Kekai's second birthday, I made a train cake, adding blue food dye to the yellow cake mix. The frosting was dark blue, thick and gooey with a vague resemblance to a midnight locomotive. Nobody else's mother called to report, but all my kids had blue poop for three days.

At eleven, my oldest daughter requested a Princess Sleepover. I made baby-doll nightgowns for all eight adorable princesses. A month before Kekoa's tenth birthday, I started tossing out themes. He adamantly refused and told me, "No themes, Mom. I mean it. Just boys, cake and games like normal kids!" That killed the vibe, so I retired from my birthday bonanzas.

I still found ways to express my inner creative spirit. I made every kid's Halloween costume for fifteen years. Both my daughters wore the mermaid costume for photo ops at various beach party event productions. I lined up in the grade-school "mom car" queue wearing a bright yellow Big Bird mask. Kekai, the youngest at seven, ran up, opened the car door and yelled for his friends to come see his super cool mom. Kekoa, almost ten, climbed in the back seat, tossed his bag on the floor, leaned over the seat and demanded, "Lose the mask, Mom!" That kid was a buzz kill.

In 2005 I rented a warehouse for my ever-increasing linen and theme decor inventory. As the kids got older, events became more elaborate. The tables at Kekai's eighth grade graduation dinner were dressed in black linen, sheer silver swirl overlays, silver lamé napkins, candelabra, black tapers and black linen chair covers with silver ties.

My high school graduation night events were legendary. For Kaleo's class of 2003, two dads and I rented Māhukona Beach Park pavilion. The parents cleaned it up and painted. I provided a bus and table decor from the good ol' Fun Express trinkets languishing in my warehouse, including kazoos, beach hats, giant sunglasses, glowing Frisbees and light sticks. I provided roundtrip mainland tickets for Pepper, a three-piece reggae band originally from Kailua-Kona, in exchange for performing. I heard the alcohol and *pakalōlō* were epic.

For Kekoa's graduation, I turned Kahuā Ranch's pavilion into a Rastafarian lounge with my event furniture, pillows, rugs and accent lighting. For Kekai's grad night, we rented Hāpuna's golf clubhouse for a red-hot dinner dance.

Each year Hawai'i Preparatory Academy's (HPA) fall Pumpkin Patch borrowed my *paniolo* entry arch, hay bales, wagon wheels and country props. Beginning in 1997, I hosted the caramel apple booth for ten years. I threw a "dipping party" two days in advance. The local grocery store donated apples, I purchased a five-gallon bucket of caramel from Kailua Candy Company and a variety of toppings: nuts, coconut flakes, gummy worms and candy corn. The kids removed the apple labels, wiped them down and cleaned up after the event. The production line featured Fran on dipping, Dave and Carol on decoration and Kulamanu as the runner, moving apples through the gauntlet and replenishing supplies as needed. Judy and Helene dominated the wrapping and decorative ties. Workers begged for invitations to the "Great Dipping" and were upset if they missed it. I supplied pizza, pūpū and margaritas. Every year, we sold out 200 caramel apples for two dollars each in scrips. Towards the end, I begged to donate $400 and call it good, but HPA would not have it. My caramel apples were a tradition! I was relieved when my last kid graduated.

One year Kaleo found a litter of kittens in the warehouse. They were orange and black, so we named them Punkin and Spook. An hour later he found two more in the same colors. We called them Deja and Boo. Cayenne promptly stuffed them down her tee shirt, balanced on her generous bosom, their little heads peeking out under her chin. I sold the kittens for one scrip each at the caramel apple booth with a sign noting their worms were free.

A Wiffle ball tournament was Waimea Rotary's major fundraiser in 1996 when I joined. It consisted of copious amounts of alcohol consumption while knocking a Wiffle ball around a Rotarian-designed course in a Parker Ranch pasture with a golf club. As a prize committee volunteer, I tapped all my suppliers and colleagues for donations. Each year, more involved, I provided linen, decor and fun giveaways leftover from the previous years' events.

In 2002 we added an Oktoberfest fundraiser as an extended drought had made the dry pastures dusty and unsafe. I invited hotel and restaurant chefs to sponsor food stations for the next five years. I once turned the Blue Dragon Restaurant into a jazz club, with props from a prom catalog. It later become a real jazz club. I placed many themed installation dinners with my hotel partners. Pukalani Stables in Waimea hosted several Halloween costume balls. Fellow Rotarian Riley Smith was my best-ever prop manager, "Just tell me what to do, Kathy!"

The treasures from my warehouse were bottomless and I themed weekly meetings near holidays. My co-Rotarians obediently enjoyed their lunch dressed in ridiculous St. Patrick's Day hats, shamrock bow ties and shiny green beads. Easter Bunny ears were a hit, as were Valentine hearts, ribbons and roses. My five-foot-tall Uncle Sam floppy doll visited on Independence Day with flags and patriotic hats for everyone.

At numerous Christmas parties, I combined my Grinch costume with a Santa beard and hat. Everyone had to sit on my lap and tell me what they wanted for Christmas. (It gave new meaning to naughty or nice.) My favorite Christmas card pictures me in costume with my little gold reading glasses perched on my nose, sipping a *li hing liliko'i* lemon drop through a straw to keep my beard clean.

I could never say no to requests for help from a nonprofit or community event. I always made my kids volunteer, too. They didn't appreciate it at all, but they were always troopers!

Santa must be a DMC!

Who else could organize Christmas Eve & still have time for Cocktails!

Santa's Li Hing Lilikoi Lemon Drop
A Sweet Martini with a Holiday Attitude

1 ½ oz. Vodka
2 oz. Sweet & Sour
Splash of Sugar Water
Splash of Lilikoi Purée
Squeeze of Fresh Lemon
Rim the glass with Li Hing Powder
Shake and serve as a Martini
Signature Drink at Kathy Clarke Hawaii!

I CANNOT RESIST A MIC

I absolutely cannot resist a microphone, especially after a glass or two of champagne. My friends and coworkers try to distract me, but it seldom works.

I was under a tent in a dry cow pasture in Waimea the first time the siren called. The emcee for our Rotary Wiffle ball fundraiser was a no-show. Someone handed me a mic and told me to get up there. I declined, but they were desperate. I poured more champagne into my red jumbo plastic cup and downed it gracefully.

"Only if I have a partner," I said, with a ladylike burp.

"Clyde, the bank manager, will co-host. He has experience."

Thus, the Clyde and Kathy show was born. Outfitted in cowboy boots, jeans and paniolo-style shirt, I straightened my hat, finished off my cup and refilled it.

"OK, here we go!" I said as I mounted the stage. Memories of that first show and auction are vague. The more outrageous I got, the more insane Clyde became. I do recall commenting on nice tushes in

Wranglers, and Clyde offered to show us his ring… which was not on his hand. People were in stitches for days, or so I was told.

My husband sat with his back to us and on the ride home, I asked him why he never turned around. "I was afraid to. I wasn't sure what would come out of your mouth next." Well, it must not have been that bad as I was invited back the next year.

Months later, while on a plane, an older couple kept turning around and looking at me, smiling big grins. As we waited to deplane, they asked, "Are you a Rotarian?"

"I am," I said proudly, thinking they recognized me from a meeting.

Nope.

"We remember you from the Wiffle ball tournament! We have never laughed so hard in our lives."

I nodded, smiled and hurriedly deplaned.

III

HAWAI'I TOURISM EVOLVES
1990–2008

1990
My fifth birth child, Kekoa (sixth child), is born at home in Waimea in July.

1991
My sixth birth child, Kekai (seventh child), is born at home in Waimea in November.

1990-1991
Savings & loan crisis begins recovery with high interest rates. Kuwait invasion and Gulf War rock the economy. Soviet Union collapses. US military stops bombing Kahoʻolawe and returns island to the state in 1993. Rupert Murdock builds Kōʻele Lodge and Mānele Bay Resort on Lānaʻi. Grand Hyatt, Four Seasons and Kea Lani hotels built in Wailea, Maui. Japanese yen begins to tank. Per HVB, visitor count is 6,723,531 and stays consistently just below 7M for the next fifteen years.

1992
Maritz signs the Ford Motor Company incentive contract and energizes their business. Ritz Carlton Kapalua is built. Pineapple production ends on Lānaʻi, and Oʻahu sugar production closes.

1992
Hurricane ʻIniki devastates Kauaʻi in September.

1993
I operate 650 pax group on devastated Kauaʻi and 1,200 pax at Waikoloa Hilton over the same dates in August. The World Wide Web, invented by computer scientist Tim Berners-Lee, comes online.

1994
Two large travel agencies merge to form Carlson Wagonlit Travel, which dominates the market for a while. Hāmākua Sugar closes.

1995-1996
Hawaiʻi tourism emerges from Gulf War slump. Kailua-Kona airport begins international flights.

1997
I operate 900 pax group at Hilton Waikoloa in December. First group rodeo at Waikōloa Stables rained out. The horses visit the hotel. I begin hiring permanent program managers.

1998
Hawaiʻi Tourism Authority (HTA) established. The Hawaiʻi Convention Center opens on Oʻahu. USS *Missouri* comes to Pearl Harbor. TAT increased from 6% to 7.25% to pay for convention center.

2000

I slip on the tile at Mauna Kea Beach Hotel while delivering Christmas cheer and break a leg. Increase office staff to six employees. Operate 45 to 55 groups per year until 2008. Y2K threat fizzles. Dot-com bubble bursts.

2001

I operate 600 and 280 pax groups back-to-back at Hilton Waikoloa in August, followed by two waves of 900 at multiple Kā'anapali hotels immediately after.

2001

September 11: World Trade Centers attacked. PRIME marketing event is operating with one hundred meeting planners in attendance on O'ahu.

2001

My staff and I make the rounds at Maui and Hawai'i hotels. Dress up sales, catering and hotel managers in Halloween costumes and take photos for Christmas calendar. We deliver calendars to hotels for Christmas promo.

2002

Reopen the Maui office on Waine'e Street. Host Fourth of July parties in Lāhainā and Waimea for industry colleagues. Linda Lingle is elected first female governor of Hawai'i. Airlines start cutting commissions for travel agents.

2003

I operate two waves of 900 and 800 pax at Hilton Waikoloa. Celebrate Thanksgiving with two Turkey Gobble events for industry colleagues on Maui and Hawai'i Island. I work my ass off for the next five years and let someone else raise my children. Iraq War begins.

2004

Four hurricanes devastate Florida and parts of southern US. Minimum wage is $5.85 and is set to increase 70¢ each year.

2005

I take my whole family (12 of us!) on vacation to Ireland. Hurricane Katrina strikes New Orleans. Hawai'i visitor counts hit 7.5M from 2005 through 2007. Apple introduces iPhone in 2007.

2006-2008

I co-chair Paniolo Preservation Society's (PPS) Waiomina Centennial Celebration taking 32 Hawaiian artisans and paniolo to Cheyenne, Wyoming, in 2008 for a cultural exchange and produce a series of events in Waimea. Stock market crashes. Visitor counts fall below 7M in 2008-2010.

RANDOM FIRSTS

In 1993 I had a client with two large simultaneous programs in Waikoloa on the Big Island and on Kaua'i. Hurricane 'Iniki had devastated Kaua'i just eleven months prior. Knowing the island would not be the lush and charming destination they booked, our client committed to helping the island by operating the first program after the hurricane.

Six hundred and fifty attendees were offered a choice of two hosted tours over three days. That's thirteen hundred seats on an island that did not have a *single* tour in operation. I began preparations in February but as August grew closer, my suppliers could not provide operating capacities or rates as insurance settlements had not been finalized and suppliers had no idea what they could rebuild. By Memorial Day, slightly panicked, I booked two condominiums in Po'ipū and took the nanny, six children under eleven and my husband to check on the tour operations. For three days we each took two children (in various combinations) and experienced tours with every supplier, sometimes doing two tours in a day. Nā Pali coast boats, snorkel catamarans and land tours—we did them all. The suppliers realized I was serious, and I needed their full cooperation.

By the fourth day, based on all my options, I knew I still did not have enough seats. I asked Rick Haviland, one of my tour operators and last hope, what his family did for fun. He said they paddled up the Hulā'ia River on lazy Sundays.

"Perfect," I said. "On Tuesday you're going to take my entire family for a paddle up the river." My two youngest were sixteen months and three years old, so I suggested he bring his daughter's life jackets. Away we went, the wind blowing us up the river on a glorious tranquil adventure past the Menehune Fish Ponds. We ran out of river and crawled up a steep muddy embankment to the road. We returned to our car in the back of a pickup truck.

"This is a tour!" I told Rick. God bless him. Once he was over the shock, he applied for permits, rounded up the other kayak companies and a new tour was born. He has expanded his business ever since. The river kayak turned out to be the group's most popular activity.

I sent Maya, the program lead, back to Kaua'i, fully equipped with paperwork and procedures to operate the program, while I stayed on the Big Island. We hired local Kaua'i ladies for the hospitality desk and their expansive aloha set the tone for the week. In true Hawaiian style, they brought food and shared it with not only our staff, but the client's staff and even the guests. They made flower lei and hair pieces for the attendees, shared local knowledge and quickly took over the tour procedures. With Maya in charge, they ran the program and handled every situation with aloha. My few regular staff were pretty much window dressing whose main job was sniffing bus diesel.

There were not enough commercial fishing boats to meet the demand so our Ladies of Aloha, manning the hospitality desk, hopped on the phone and in no time we had all the fishing slots filled. The boats came with locally "catered" lunches and beverages, provided by the owners. When the taxi company did not have enough vehicles to transfer our attendees, husbands showed up in vans to take our guests where they needed to go. We were compelled to advise our client that these were not registered taxis or Coast Guard licensed boats, but she only laughed and said, "I am so glad you were able to accommodate our attendees," and walked away. Betty Savage has always been my favorite client.

In 1999, I created a variation on the river kayak tour. Two hundred and fifty attendees paddled up the river, Rick's guides led them on a short waterfall hike to a meadow on Kipu Ranch. They enjoyed lunch under Fred Atkins's giant tent before motor coaches returned them to the hotel. Not one to let a good venue go to waste, my next group of forty guests paddled and hiked to the meadow. The client had donated twenty *'ukulele* to Hanalei School and the class performed and enjoyed lunch with their benefactors. Helicopters landed in the meadow and flew our guests on a waterfall tour before returning them to the Princeville heliport.

I was hung up on ranches for a while, always looking for creative uses of our natural resources. In 1997, I planned the first group interactive rodeo at Waikōloa Stables. We were rained out, but the rodeo horses came to visit at the Hyatt (Hilton) Waikoloa.

In 2006, I placed the first 1,300 attendees at Kualoa Ranch on Oʻahu with lunch and a choice of tours including ATV, horseback, Jeep jungle, fishpond and botanical garden tours. In 2008, at Kahuā Ranch on the Big Island, I hosted 350 pax for lunch and a choice of ATV, horseback or a scenic ranch tour aboard a Pinzgauer all-terrain vehicle. I added thirty-minute waterfall helicopter tours to future Kahuā groups. In 2011, we revisited Kualoa Ranch with 1,200 guests for lunch and tours.

Helicopters were my passion. In 2004, using ten helicopters, I coordinated four hundred pax on a ten-minute waterfall tour off the great lawn at Maui Tropical Plantation. It was as beautiful and smooth as the Maui Waltz and in ninety-five minutes we had flown everyone. In 2006, I chartered the first helicopter to land my VIP attendees on chef Bev Gannon's front lawn in Makawao, Maui. On the Big Island, thirty guests flew a volcano helicopter tour and landed next to a remote waterfall on Kohala Mountain just before sunset, where they enjoyed a gourmet wine-pairing dinner. After dark, four-wheel drive vans transported them off the mountain. The potentially rainy February evening was perfect except for a small whirligig that dusted our participants and their plates with the wood chips used to cover up the mud spots. You learn something new at every event!

As expected, competitors duplicated the many events I created for my clients, but I didn't mind. Someone had to break the sound barrier and my list of exciting "firsts" is long and varied!

THE SACRIFICE

Shortly after we moved to Waimea, my young children were raised by nannies and, indirectly, my employees. At one time I had seven employees in the remodeled "virgin" garage, so named as it had never seen a car. Half my staff were named on the kids' medical emergency authorizations.

When Kekoa was seven years old, he stayed home with a fever. I left my desk for coffee, and upon returning, I started to tuck my legs under my solid oak desk only to find little Kekoa scrunched up underneath with a comforter and a pillow. "Koa, what are you doing down there?" I asked. His sad face looked up at me. "I don't feel good, Mom. I just want to be close to you."

As teenagers, the kids would file through the office to see Mom and "her workers" as they called them. Kawehi would strut shirtless through the office in soccer shorts and cleats, way too buff for a high schooler and completely aware of his charming good looks. Fran, my middle-aged *hapa*-Japanese bookkeeper, complained, "I am too old to see that kind of talent up close!"

Cayenne, a middle-schooler, greeted everyone with a joyful smile, a kind word or a funny nickname, then sang her way into the main house. Kekai, the youngest, danced by with a wicked grin. Kekoa teased the ladies and dodged hugs.

Before Dave, my operations manager, began working in the Waimea office, he tutored my "middle-middle" child in third-grade math. Every time Kaleo got a problem right, Dave slid an M&M across the desk as a reward. Later, Dave kept little round plastic-wrapped "safeties" in his desk drawer and let the boys know to help themselves. He never offered them to my girls! After a three-day company retreat at the Sheraton (now Fairmont Orchid) he and Carol, one of my program managers, fell in love and lived happily ever after.

One year a last-minute client insisted she wanted her proposal before Christmas to review over the holidays. I finished it on Christmas Eve while my family hung stockings and drank champagne in the main house. I followed up in January and she apologized for not having time to review it. I never let a client do that again. "No" was an answer. Unless I was off island or operating a program, I never missed a holiday, soccer game, play, teacher meeting or a child-related event again.

IOU

One of my program managers followed me out of the office as I was headed for the airport.

"Do you have a sec?" she asked.

"Sure, but I do have to run. What do you need?"

"My husband and I are buying a house and we need twenty thousand dollars in the bank to qualify for the loan." Her face was tense and pensive.

I paused and exclaimed, "My dear, you don't leave me much time!"

I turned around, walked back into the office, wrote a check for the amount, scribbled "I Owe You $20K" on a piece of paper for her to sign and date, then rushed off to the airport. She paid me back a few months later. I'm a big believer in trusting your gut and your people.

MARKETING REINVENTED

Over the years, I have shamelessly taken advantage of my children's talents. Christmas is one of my favorite hotel marketing holidays. My beautiful middle child, Cayenne, began singing a cappella Christmas carols in her three-and-a-half octave range beginning in her teens. Her beautiful voice echoed in lobbies, hallways and hotel sales and catering offices. When she sang "O Holy Night," people cried.

In 2018, arriving at the Fairmont Orchid while working our way through the hotels, we went straight to the catering office on the main floor, not realizing the department had moved and the space was now occupied by the general manager. I flamboyantly burst in, full of holiday cheer and the GM's assistant, appalled, asked if she could help me.

"Of course!" I laughed. "We're here to sing Christmas carols! Where is everyone?"

I didn't recognize the GM sitting at the only other desk. Doreen, my longtime friend, now the head of HR, was obviously meeting with him when we barged in. She jumped up and, like coming home, we shared a long hug that only old friends can appreciate.

She introduced us to the GM and not breaking stride, Cayenne blessed them with a very special Christmas gift in her exceptionally beautiful voice. The GM gave us a warm embrace and said, "I was not feeling the spirit of the season, but you have just given me back Christmas."

For years, I continued to use holidays as an excuse to stop by the hotel's sales and catering offices. I found fun themed "gifts" to present with flair and flourish. One Valentine's Day, we delivered red mini mailboxes filled with Valentine candy. Fourth of July was easy with small red, white and blue pails filled with pencils, hard candy and flying tiny flags. One year I bought 850 chocolate bunnies from the local youth group fundraiser, put on my pink and white bunny ears and distributed them around the islands. Green pinwheels, lucky charms, shamrock-decorated slap bracelets and leprechaun characters for St. Patrick's Day. We changed the holiday celebrations and giveaways each year.

Halloween always held great potential. After September 11, 2001, the hotels were receiving cancellations as fast as the phone could ring. Everyone was operating from fear and uncertainty. The hotel sales staff watched their bonuses and commissions evaporate. Hotels began cutting back as revenues fell. The trickle down was severe and Hawai'i, dependent on tourism, was crumbling.

I had not yet laid off staff and was determined to go forward with our Halloween hotel blitz. We filled big plastic tubs with wearable Halloween paraphernalia

including crazy witch or wizard hats, pumpkin hats, Cat in the Hat stripes, green and pink flourescent wigs, eyeglasses with Groucho mustaches, animal noses, sequin-rimmed glasses, vampire teeth, big red plastic lips, rubber witch claws, feather boas and tiaras. My staff and I were relentless as we pulled costumes from the bucket and dressed up everyone in the office. No one got away from us, including several GMs who wandered by. When they were decked out in their finest Halloween attire, we took a group picture. Like Waldo, I was in every photo! Then we whisked ourselves out the door, leaving them all dressed up and laughing as we waved goodbye.

We visited all hotels on Maui and Hawai'i Island. Our highest compliment came from Joanie at the Mauna Lani. *We gave her hope,* she told us. They were so depressed over the cancellations, and I brought laughter back into their lives. She said, "You don't know how wonderful it felt to laugh again."

In 2002, I patriotically threw Fourth of July parties on Maui and Hawai'i Island. In 2003 we celebrated Thanksgiving with fall parties and a turkey gobble competition. In 2005 I celebrated twenty-five years in business with an industry event at 'Anaeho'omalu Bay on Hawai'i Island. Well over a hundred and fifty industry colleagues made the trip to Waikoloa, Willie K entertained, and my next decade began.

NOTHING IS IMPOSSIBLE

In 2007, Hawai'i incentive programs were the ultimate reward to motivate US company sales teams to peak performance. The rest of the world was still catching on, so I was cautious when Hector, the owner of a major medical pharmaceutical company from Caracas, Venezuela, contacted me. His charming, bombastic style won me over.

As a reward for achieving the company's goals, he brought all three hundred employees to Los Angeles for a ball game, then flew to Hawai'i for three days at the Hilton Waikoloa. The group was young, full of excitement and knew how to party, as did Hector. After an extravagant lū'au, the awards featured each recipient on a ten-by-seventeen-foot IMAG screen. Extravagant fireworks followed, and an after-hours DJ extended the evening. The next day, Brett Smith from BGS staged a "Rickety Rackety Raft" team-building event followed by a very competitive regatta in the hotel's lagoon. Another wild evening lasted until dawn.

The following morning, the employees showed up at 6:30 a.m. for their circle island volcano tour. Off they went, hungover but happy.

Around 9:30 a.m., Hector called my office. In his delightful accent, and a slow gravelly voice, he said, "Katty, everyone has left on the volcano tour."

"Yes, Hector. Everyone showed up and they're on their way." I paused. "Hector, did you miss the bus?"

"Yes, Katty. I think I had a very good time last night. But I need to be with my people now."

"Hector, they're gone. They are three hours ahead of you and at the volcano by now."

"I know, Katty. But can you get me there? I need to be with them."

"Hector, it's over a two-hour drive to the volcano."

"Yes, Katty, can you get me there? Money is not a consideration." He was determined.

My brain went into overdrive as I quickly reviewed options to make this happen. "My dearest Hector, yes. I can get you there—please be ready to leave in the next twenty minutes and stay close to your cell phone. I will call you back."

I contacted Sunshine Helicopters and promised to deliver Hector shortly for a direct flight to Hilo. I sent a car for Hector and called him back.

"Hector, be in the lobby in ten minutes. A car will pick you up and take you to the heliport. The driver has your name. They will fly you to Hilo where another car will take you to the lunch location. The group will be arriving there in an hour, and you can greet them as they arrive. You can ride home with your people."

"Oh, Katty, that is wonderful, wonderful!" I could hear the relief and excitement in his voice as he continued to thank me extensively in Spanish. "I love you!"

As much I appreciated his thanks, I had to interrupt. "Hector, you need to get down to the lobby! I love you too, but please hurry!"

Doing the impossible and making your client happy does not get better than that.

THE GREAT WAIOMINA

In 1908, Eben Low, a ranch owner, traveled by steamship and railroad with Hawaiian cowboys Ikua Purdy, Archie Kaʻaua and his brother Jack Low to compete in a world roping competition in Cheyenne, Wyoming. Our Big Island paniolo took first, third and sixth place, respectively.

Ikua Purdy, the "Last Cowboy Standing," roped a steer in fifty-six seconds, on a borrowed horse. The first non-Wyomingite to win the competition, Ikua and his fellow paniolo taught those Wyoming cowboys how to rope! In 2007, he was inducted into the Cheyenne Frontier Days (CFD) Hall of Fame and the National Cowboy Museum Rodeo Hall of Fame in 1999.

In 2006, the Waimea Paniolo Preservation Society began a three-year project to commemorate the one-hundred-year anniversary of this momentous accomplishment. Keawe Vredenburg, Dr. Billy Bergin and I co-chaired the project. During several advance visits to Cheyenne, we met with CFD Committee Chairs and city officials, established Waimea and Cheyenne as sister cities, attended receptions, meetings and events. In 2007, I brought my youngest son, Kekai, and my oldest daughter, Cinnamon, who performed hula in paniolo attire for the Cheyenne Chamber of Commerce.

In July 2008, I managed flights to Cheyenne, rental cars and rooms at the historic Plains Hotel for thirty-two Hawaiian paniolo and artisans for a cultural exchange. Throughout the week, we coordinated interactive performances of our musicians, artisans and cultural practitioners, which included lauhala weaving, lei making, Hawaiian saddle making, feather work (*lei hulu*), *pāʻū* wrap demos and talk-story. We rode in parades, demonstrated the traditional Hawaiian rodeo technique Poʻo Wai U in the arena, exchanged chants and hula with Native Americans and shared our culture and aloha with the CFD visitors and residents of Cheyenne. The Old West Museum developed a seasonal exhibit based on our 1908 roping triumph and strong historical town connection that became a permanent museum display. My daughter, Cayenne, at twenty-three, came along as my only travel staff and opened events singing "Hoʻonani I Ka Makua Mau," a beautiful Hawaiian prayer and sang the "Star-Spangled Banner" for the entire CFD committee at the final aloha reception, her voice echoing through the museum halls.

Returning to Waimea, we continued celebrations with a Cultural Family Day and reception at Anna Ranch, a reenactment of Old Hawaiʻi on horseback, trail rides, a black and white gala dinner at Puʻuopelu (the Parker Ranch homestead), a cowgirl lunch and fashion show featuring famous Hawaiian designer Nakeʻu, a Melveen Leed concert and a final *mahalo paʻina*. Events were my thing, after all!

The centennial celebration brought awareness throughout the state of the Big Island's rich paniolo heritage, which is honored front and center in Waimea with a bronze statue of Ikua Purdy on horseback roping his steer. The twenty-seven-foot-long, sixty-five-ton sculpture by well-known Arizona-based cowboy artist Fred Fellows was placed at Parker Ranch Center in 2006. At the Waimea Town Center, a giant painted boot, donated by Dr. Billy and Patricia Bergin, portrays the Hawaiian paniolo in action. In 2009 the governor declared "The Year of the Paniolo." Better late than never!

HERDING CATS

It is well known in the visitor industry that attendees lose all common sense as soon as they step on an airplane. They arrive in paradise and are suddenly unable to string three coherent thoughts together. They leave valuables and tickets in the plane's seat pocket. They walk right past their company name on a ten-by-fourteen sign, then call the event planner in a panic because no one is there to greet them. The irate planner calls us, and we track them down at baggage claim. They cannot keep track of their bags, belongings or time.

A lovely group on Maui rented cars instead of securing transfers. Our staff greeted them and sent the driver off to pick up the car while we assisted their travel companion with luggage. We placed the companion with bags on the curb, having instructed the driver to swing back around for pick up. This worked well until we noticed several familiar bags abandoned on the curb. A nametag check confirmed they were our group. We sent the bags to the hotel and later asked our sweet, elderly attendees why they left their bags sitting on the curb.

"You had taken such good care of us, we thought you would handle the bags as well!"

Right!

Asking Ms. Lucy to ID her bag before loading the bus, she pointed to a blue suitcase. The name tag was *not* Ms. Lucy's. She pointed to another bag...also not hers. She had no idea what her luggage looked like. We found her black bag and called our airport staff to be on guard.

Our favorite attendees checked their bags through to Honolulu but forgot their final destination was an outer island. Sometimes they didn't know there was more than one island. Today, the airlines link flights but back then it was common to track down a "short-checked" bag.

What part of "put your name on your luggage" is so hard? Fortunately, travel staff are detectives par excellence. Sadie Hawkins borrowed her married sister's suitcase tagged as Mrs. Susie Cream-Cheese. But of course, we intuitively knew that it was really Sadie's! On another occasion, a travel staff put the VIP's luggage in her rental car trunk for transport from the airport. The hotel ransacked their property for three days before the staff remembered it was still in the trunk.

GOOD CLIENT SLIPS

As my children were growing up, we wanted to recognize good behavior and discourage bad. I came up with Good Kid Slips. An act of kindness, doing chores or feeding the dog without being asked, helping a sibling with homework or other good deeds received a slip with color pictures of flowers, rainbows, kitties, kites, soccer balls and balloons. Later I used each kids' picture so no one could inadvertently misappropriate a slip. "I Goofed" Kid Slips were always purple, with oil cans, snakes, rats and ugly monsters. Good Kid Slips were cashed in for treats, movie time or special privileges. As a cautionary tale, I often reminded my children there were at least seven common species whose mothers devour their young, and prudence is certainly a virtue.

I would love to try this incentive with my clients. Good Client Slips, decorated with colorful Hawaiian flowers, hula dancers and palm trees could be earned for reasonable lead time or manifests in Excel and redeemed for Hawaiian mac nuts, chocolate-covered coffee beans or other treats. There could even be a monetary discount for actually reading the contract!

Client Goof Slips, with scary jellyfish and mean-looking sharks, would be awarded for poor planning, last-minute panic requests, asking for free services or insisting they do their own centerpieces. All Client Goof Slips would be charged a proportional "Grief Tax" added on the final bill.

IV

INSIDE HAWAI'I TOURISM 2009–2022

2008
Close Maui office. Downsize Waimea office. Great Recession due to mortgage crisis. Minimum wage is $7.25. Aloha Airlines shuts down.

2009
Hawaiian Airlines marks 80th anniversary.

2010-2012
Work my ass off to get out of recession debt. All kids in college or on their own. I invite my spouse to leave, permanently. 2011 visitor count increases to 7,174,397 and continues to grow. Instagram is launched. First TSA PreCheck implemented at Las Vegas airport.

2012
Larry Ellison of Oracle purchases island of Lāna'i from Murdock.

2013
My son Kekoa graduates from the Air Force Academy.

2014-2015
Kekoa crashes his motorcycle, sustaining a severe traumatic brain injury (TBI). I live in Colorado for over a year and run my business remotely with occasional commutes.

2017
In July, I break my leg again at Waimea post office, drive myself to ER. Marriott acquires Starwood and becomes world's largest hotel company.

2018-2019
I balance my life, close my warehouse, downsize my business. Visitor counts increase year over year to 10,243,165 visitors in 2019. Visitor spending falls 3.5% as visitor quality declines. Residents become weary of tourism.

2020-2021
The Great COVID-19 Shut Down devastates Hawai'i tourism. TAT increases to 10.248%. *I write my first book about my unconventional life. It's published in December 2021..*

2020
On Mother's Day, my 88-year-old mother passes away. In October, I fall and break my leg again after only two margaritas at the Brew House in Waimea.

2022
In January, Hawai'i counties add a 3% county accommodations tax. Screws up everyone's budgets and hurts small business. Pent-up visitor demand floods Hawai'i's debilitated businesses. *I write a second book (this one!).*

STAFF MEETING

In May 2014, I received the dreaded five a.m. phone call. My twenty-four-year-old son, a recent Air Force Academy graduate, was fighting for his life after a near-fatal motorcycle accident. I flew from Kona and arrived in Colorado Springs less than twenty-four hours after the accident. When Kekoa's condition finally stabilized, I came home for a three-day weekend to organize the business for a prolonged absence before returning to Colorado. I welcomed the weekend distraction to rescue my empty house from neglect and tried to normalize the fear and uncertainty I felt for my life and my son's future.

My staff was miraculous during my absence—I was blessed to have their support. My business office, a garage connected to the main house via an overstocked pantry, had been an extension of my home for over thirty-five years. Although my staff was in and out of my home and home office regularly, Bobo the cat was the sole tenant during my six-weeks-plus absence.

Bobo spent his alone time depositing multiple mice in the pantry hall so my most mouse-shy staff member could practice screaming hysterically and jumping up on chairs while flapping her hands. I laughed when they shared the image, as she is six feet tall, raised in Waiʻanae and a certified "don't-mess-with-me" tita.

One early morning, she stood on the chair for half an hour until her co-worker arrived to flush the dead mouse down the toilet. After a few days, Kulamanu, the pragmatic disposer, had to start taking the mice to the dump on her way home as she had a recurring nightmare that the toilet would back up and those mice would haunt her in a most unpleasant way. She put them in sandwich baggies and tossed them out the car window as she drove by the bins, barely slowing down. Bobo finally ran out of mice sometime in late August and my favorite tita resumed her normal early-morning arrival.

DEAR CLIENT, DID YOU READ THE CONTRACT?

There is a certain level of sainthood required in managing clients. One must maintain a sense of humor, learn to forgive miscues and meet challenges with patience. In my younger days I dove in with enthusiasm, ready to make their wildest harebrained fantasies a reality. No stone unturned, no call unmade, no supplier's patience limit left untested in pursuit of fulfilling a request. How many times have I heard, *I really need to give my VIP something unique and different that they can't do or buy themselves?*

Every young planner knows everything and is essentially planning their wedding with a color palette of pastels or dramatic color contrasts, clipped from multiple wedding sites. When advised Hawai'i's linen inventory is limited and shipping from the mainland is expensive, they will impatiently demand you stick to the vision and insist you find a solution in their budget. The "team" will review the proposal (as no one is ever in charge) and select a locally sourced, bland tan with a textured burlap overlay belonging to someone else's wedding concept. A florist they find online will provide accents in everyone's wedding colors. Advised the VIP cannot stand in front of the speakers and hold a mic without producing ear-shattering feedback, the client will go ballistic and tell you to "Fix it!" while the "Team Leader" stands, arms folded, with a condemning glare because you were unable to defy science. You will begin to pray for the older, more experienced, planners on future programs. On occasion, I had the urge to let clients run with their bad idea, watch as disaster unfolded and wondered if I would feel guilty. I never found out.

Each outlandish request produced extraordinary creative adventures or, when necessary, subtle redirection. However, there are a few responses I *wished* I could have made but didn't!

> *Dear Client, I understand the Director of Marketing is bringing his mistress, but they have separate rooms. His wife will be arriving for the farewell gala, and you need my assistance in making sure she is seated at the staff table. Can you clarify if you want the wife or the mistress seated with the staff?*

> *Dear Client, I was not able to secure a dinner reservation for sixteen guests tonight at seven at an oceanfront restaurant within walking distance. What, exactly, are you smoking?*

> *Dear Client, we will be charging for a lead staff during your program although you won't let them sit at the hospitality desk. Our Hawai'i staff are,*

sadly, adept at hiding in the bushes to operate a program so your client never finds out that we are the ones who do all the work, coordinating tours, transportation and events. We do charge double, however for the embarrassment.

Dear Client, yes, the staff are necessary. We don't provide product without service. Period. Please don't ask again.

Dear Client, I am sorry the sailboat could not sail during the charter due to lack of wind. No, we will not refund your money.

Dear Client, we cannot cancel the snorkel sail seventy-two hours out because you just realized you did not get enough sign-ups. Please read the terms of service in my contract that you signed.

Dear Client, the night manta dive generally departs at sunset which is just before it gets dark. The mantas are not active in the daytime so we cannot move the tour to an earlier time.

Dear Client, your three-hundred-pound guest cannot go on the zipline which has a two-hundred-fifty-pound weight limit. And FYI, rhinestone-encrusted sandals are not classified as closed-toed shoes.

Dear Client, no, your attendee cannot take their child on the zipline tour in a baby backpack.

Dear Client, we cannot transfer your boss's two-year-old child without a car seat. (I must remember to add that to the contract terms.)

Dear Client, it is unfortunate that the bus you chartered directly (without our help, to save a dollar) broke down and you were late for your dinner reservation.

Dear Client, since you booked the private room directly with the restaurant and declined our assistance to save another buck, I am unable to call them, change the menu or alter the guest count. Not my monkey, not my circus.

Dear Client, we have spent months professionally developing the theme and components for your formal awards dinner. I cannot provide my florist contact so the VIPs' wives can make cheap, amateur centerpieces.

Dear Client, mahalo for sending your flight manifest as a PDF. The administrative charge to convert it to Excel (so we can sort it) is fifty-five dollars per hour, with minimum four hours. Please refer to our contract where we explain this in detail.

Dear Client, I am sorry your attendee did not read the departure notice provided. It clearly states the hotel departure time and confirms the flight information. The bus left on time. I suggest your attendee sashay out to the front entrance with their bags and hope there is a taxi within thirty minutes they can hire, at their own expense, or we can transfer them and charge you back plus a 35% service fee. If they miss the flight, they cannot come back as the hotel is sold out and there's another group right behind yours.

Dear Client, I have now revised your program components eight times. Your inability to make a final decision is wearing thin. Please see the "excessive revisions" clause in the contract.

Dear Client, apologies but we cannot handle your program of twenty-four attendees since you already booked the catamaran directly and are doing all your events through the hotel. You want help with airport transfers and random tour sales only, but don't want to pay for our staff. We are NOT a nonprofit company. Go away.

I have always been confounded by people who are oblivious to common sense. If a bucket has a hole in it, why do they think it will carry water? Sometimes, even duct tape cannot fix stupid.

Conversely, there are many clients who are treasures, and I would not trade them for the world. You know who you are!

EXPERIENCE AND WISDOM

Experience

- Prepare every proposal with care. Proof your work, double check times, dates, pax counts, inclusions and locations. Don't screw up the costing!

- Make sure the client expectations and supplier delivery match. If they don't, *fix it*. This is not optional.

- Be organized. Think in outlines. Final timelines are *not* suggestions. None of this is optional.

- Multitask on multiple levels simultaneously. If you can't do that, hire someone who can or find a new career.

- Love Excel. Get really, really good at it. Prevents wrinkles.

- Only you and the production company know you could have improved the event. Few clients have enough expertise, and they seldom have the budget anyway.

- When you have no schematic, show up early and tell your supplier where you want things placed. It's called "Point and Shoot," per Jonathan.

- Keep event inventory sheets. Learn how to load and unload a prop truck.

- Counting heads is important. I once lost a Big Island bike tour attendee who fell behind, decided to bike to Kailua-Kona, met some jolly fellows, had more than a few beers, watched the sunset and hitched a ride back to the hotel (sans the bike), happy as a lark! No one had missed him.

- You are only as good as your last event.

Wisdom

- Your suppliers are your most valuable resources; an extension of yourself. Treat them well, be nice and understanding. Favors and respect are an even trade. Trust them to do their magic. There are no backups if you throw them under the bus.

- Respect your staff and give them the tools they need to take pride in their work. Never hand out incomplete information to your travel staff and expect them to wing it. That is just not fair!

- Don't micromanage your staff. If you don't trust them, don't hire them!

- Pick up the phone. It will *not* bite you, and you will get the answer you need faster. It will also improve your relationship with the callee.

- The client is not the enemy. No matter how much they are driving you crazy. They pay your bills.

- Exercise common sense. Find other people who have it. Hang out with them. It will lower your stress levels.

- Practice patience! You will need it.

- Maintain a sense of humor. You will need it.

- You are only as good as the people who support you.

- Ethics: Don't give kickbacks. They set a very bad precedent.

- Integrity: Never lose it, it cannot be regained.

- You can't fix stupid. Just accept it.

HAWAI'I'S OLDEST LIVING DMC

For the first fifteen years in business, I operated ten to twenty programs per year as the Lone Ranger, occasionally adding temporary assistants and hiring freelance travel staff. Preferring to fly under the radar, I chose to work from home and raise my children (however haphazardly) while my competitors dominated Oʻahu and grew high-profile companies.

By 1998, I had more business than I could handle on my own and hired two full-time staff. By 2002, with six new operations and office staff, I reopened the Maui office and operated forty-five to fifty-five programs per year until the 2008 recession final hit Hawaiʻi in 2009 and shot a hole in the travel industry. I was not cut out to be a boss, and managing six revolving employees for ten years was exasperating. As a perfectionist, with little innate patience, I was too driven, too autocratic and too demanding. I never relaxed my standards or my expectations. I became more and more cynical. My good friend, Diana Dorr, took me out to dinner and graciously pointed out my bad attitude. I endeavored to fix it.

By 2006, attrition was my friend! One employee gave notice. I congratulated her on her decision and wished her well. "You mean you're not going to ask me to stay?" she asked incredulously.

"No," I said, barely containing my joy. Two weeks later, another staff gave notice. Under my desk, my toes curled in delight! Stress was rolling off my shoulders! I booted out a troublemaker soon after and let the next one down easy. Ahhh, relief! My attitude was improving daily.

Visitor counts were almost seven million in 2010. I was happy with three employees, operating twenty-five to thirty-five groups each year. I quit working twenty-four-seven. With the last two children in high school, I realized I had missed the childhoods of seven beautiful human beings.

Over the last five years, many people have asked when I plan to retire. I didn't know why it was such a hot topic. Were they hoping I would go away, quietly into the night and throw my clients to the winds for harvesting? Was I looking old and tired like I *should* retire? Was I just annoying? In 2017, my own staff began hounding me about my future plans. *How long was I going to work? Did I have an exit plan?* Did they want to take over the business and were too timid to ask? I assured them résumé revisions were not imminent. It was exceedingly irritating and, frankly, no one's business. I did not replace the remaining staff as they moved on and by 2018, I retained only one administrative assistant. I stopped soliciting new business and enjoyed my repeat clients.

Visitor counts continued to increase year over year with more than ten million visitors in 2019. In the spring of that year, I closed my 3,500-square-foot prop warehouse, selling thousands of upscale table linen, napkins and chair covers. Anything of value was sold and I gave away as much as my colleagues would take—fishbowls, votives, paniolo and beach props. I sold the crazy themed paraphernalia at garage sales. Six taxidermy-dried frogs, dressed in mariachi band attire and clutching mini-instruments went to the local veterinarian. I donated reams of colored paper and supplies to the local charter school and youth programs. I was down to ten programs per year when I released my last employee. Freedom has always been my favorite word.

A year later, COVID-19 descended on the world and the bottom fell out of Hawai'i's travel industry. I had fortuitously downsized the year before. Not my first industry crisis, my heart broke for my tour operators, restaurateurs and suppliers as they terminated equipment leases, laid off staff, struggled to survive or closed entirely. Hotels temporarily shut down; businesses applied for relief. I watched from the sidelines as the top industry in Hawai'i screeched to a halt.

In the midst of the two-year restrictions and shutdowns, we remembered how much we loved our islands. When not desperately trying to keep a business alive, we suddenly found time to enjoy the beaches, the cool upcountry volcano slopes, traffic-free streets, uncrowded stores and restaurants. We planted gardens, remodeled rooms, worked on neglected projects, wrote books, enjoyed our friends and families, however remotely, and many returned to the mainland. The travel industry, as a whole, kept contact with colleagues and clients in hopes of a resurrection. We held our breath.

. . .

In 2020, HTA mandated an action plan, but each island bureau chapter did the heavy lifting to proactively implement Destination Management Action Plans (DMAP). Plans varied by island but included educating visitors on Hawaiian culture and traditions, hoping to inspire good manners, integrating community and visitor experience, protecting cultural sites and natural resources and improving infrastructure.

The targeted, well-thought-out and practical plans hope to have a positive future effect on the industry. Implementation will be the key. Visitors will continue to come to Hawai'i, in spite of having the highest visitor taxes in the world. Hopefully, our communities will embrace a new, better-behaved visitor, proactively support our Hawaiian culture in daily life and once again embrace the travel industry as an intrinsic part of our state's identity. More importantly, we must strengthen the true sense of aloha that resides precariously in our hearts without reservation. For now, a healthy Hawai'i economy will continue to depend on tourism and Hawai'i must pledge to rejuvenate from within.

. . .

I spent forty-five years influencing the hospitality and travel industry, innovating operations and policy, and creating new concepts and ideas. I mentored and trained hundreds of suppliers and staff. Many went on to advanced careers. The HVCB referred young, inexperienced planners for my patient mentorship. I created new tours and events, found and developed new venues. I promoted Hawai'i tourism and culture, supported multiple marketing events hosted by the HVCB and other industry organizations in Hawai'i, internationally and on the mainland US. Those marketing events were often my favorite projects! I didn't know how to "sell," I could only share my knowledge and aloha with friends old and new.

I never hesitated to offer my opinion, solicited or not. I lent my expertise and support to community projects, from supplying bamboo chairs for the Annual Hospice Tea to producing a life-saving fundraiser for a friend. All my life I have mentored, innovated and influenced my industry in this amazing place others love to visit but I am blessed to call home.

I was considering retirement in late 2022 but was awarded a program with three back-to-back waves of eight hundred attendees for 2023. I simply could not say no. So here I am, still running the longest-operating DMC in the state. Even at my age, the only thing I love more than making a difference, is a challenge.

Stand by for updates.

ACKNOWLEDGMENTS

It would be impossible to list everyone who made my success possible. If you don't see your name, know you are in my heart.

My incredible event partners who taught me everything I know and always went above and beyond: Hoku Damaso, Jeanne Nakagawa, Chef Bev Gannon, Bob Schwager, all the Envisions Entertainment Crew—Wayne, Herb, Wil, Kim, Ruthie, Wanda, Stephanie, Missy, Sandi and their steadfast production crews. Derek Higa and the Show Systems Hawai'i crew. So many supplier partners, but especially Paul Morris who never said no to my crazy ideas and performed miracles on demand.

HVCB meetings staff: Adele Tasaka, Kathy Dever, Debbie Hogan and Sherry Duong; so many miles traveled together, full of laughter and certainly book worthy!

A very short list of my many favorite clients: Betty Savage, Jim Ball, Steve Chapman, Lynette Wineland, Melissa Deleon, Diana Brown, Chrissy Ruiz, Robina Wahid, Baron Derr, Todd Gabello, Cathy Ewing and

Dawn Peck. You all made a difference in my life, and I would come out of retirement for all of you.

My hotel partners, too many to list. Your support over the years is sincerely appreciated and I treasure you all! Especially Brian Lynx, my favorite brother from another mother, who drove us from Wailea to Lahaina at 110 mph in his hot convertible sports car on a star-filled night.

My travel staff: Warren, Lennie, Lani, Mapuana, Pat, Melinda, Dennis, Bill, Cloy, Nalani, Nan, Tamara, Joni, Lisa and so many from the early days. They are the source of aloha, true professionals and the foundation of my success.

Kulamanu, my longest employee who got fired the most often, but always had my back. Judy Folk, my neighbor and reader who literally chases the cows and goats out of our yards in the middle of the night. Cayenne, my daughter, my biggest cheerleader and my reader who calls me *comma-tastic* because she is obsessed with the Oxford comma, and I am not! Special mahalo to all my kids who never told anyone who their mother was or expected any special treatment as they worked or played in the travel industry and were profoundly amused when people said, "Your mother is really *Kathy Clarke*?"

GLOSSARY

All translated words are Hawaiian in origin, unless indicated otherwise. Hawaiian words do not take English plural forms; for example, "lei" is both the singular and plural form.

Amfac – A land development company in Hawaiʻi, also involved in agricultural sugar and retail, with numerous "also known as" companies, Kāʻanapali Maui Beach Resort being one. One of Hawaiʻi's "Big Five" companies.

AMEX – Industry acronym for American Express Travel.

Castle & Cooke – Agriculture, food processing and real estate company, aka Dole Foods. One of Hawaiʻi's "Big Five" companies.

Codeshares – An agreement between airlines to sell seats on each other's flights.

Dine arounds – An evening of company-hosted dinners, including transportation, at multiple restaurants.

DMC – Destination Management Company; designation from the visitors' industry for a company that handles transportation, tours, event production, team building, entertainment, dinners and a wide variety of services for meeting and incentive groups. There are DMCs all over the world that specialize in specific regions and countries.

FIT – Free Independent Traveler; someone who booked their own travel plans or used a travel agent. Not associated with a group tour.

Haole – Foreigner; in modern use, a white-skinned person. Commonly thought to originate from "hā" (breath) and "'ōle" (without), in other words, "without breath."

Hapa – Half; commonly refers to persons of biracial or mixed ancestry.

HTA – Hawai'i Tourism Authority; established in 1998 by the Hawai'i State Legislature to oversee tourism marketing, branding and integration of Hawaiian cultural, natural resources and community.

HVB / HVCB – Hawai'i Visitors Bureau; changed in 1998 to Hawai'i Visitor and Convention Bureau.

IMAG – Short for "Image Magnification." Live-streaming video projection on a large screen.

MCI – Meeting and Incentive Industry; specific segment of the travel industry that specializes in corporate and association meetings and events.

Kahoʻolawe – Forty-five-square-mile uninhabited island, west of Maui. Used as a bombing target by the US Navy until returned to the state.

Kolohe – Rascal.

KBOA – Kāʻanapali Beach Operators Association; later renamed Kāʻanapali Beach Resort Association.

Lauhala – Pandanus leaf used to weave traditional Hawaiian hats, baskets and other items.

LK&P Railroad – Lahaina, Kāʻanapali & Pacific Railroad; narrow gauge train used to transport sugar cane to Pioneer Mill in Lahaina. Became a tourist attraction in 1969, closed in 2014.

MVB – Maui Visitors Bureau, aka Maui County Visitors Bureau. Later rebranded to Maui Visitors & Convention Bureau. Each county has its own bureau chapter.

Ofuro – The polite or formal term for a Japanese tub used in ritualistic soaking; informal: furo.

ʻŌpū – Belly, stomach.

Pāʻina – Party.

Pakalōlō – Marijuana aka Maui Wowie.

Paniolo – Hawaiian cowboy.

Pāʻū – Skirt; traditional fabric wrap worn by women on horseback to keep their underclothing dust free.

Pax – Common travel industry abbreviation for passengers or attendees.

Poʻo Wai U – Traditional roping technique, unique to Hawaiʻi, used by a single roper to secure cattle.

PHH – Industry acronym for Pleasant Hawaiian Holidays.

Princess Pupule – A lively, naughty hula about a Hawaiian princess who loves to give away her papayas. In Hawaiian, pupule means crazy, reckless or wild; pronounced poo-poo-lay (rhymes with "give away").

Pūpū – Appetizers.

Site inspection – When a potential client visits the destination to assess suitable hotels, tours and services before committing to a contract.

TAT – Transient Accommodation Tax; first implemented in Hawaiʻi in 1987.

Tita – Hawaiian slang word for sister; usually a sassy, precocious or tough girl.

ʻUhane – Soul, spirit or ghost.

In the late 1970s, Kathy Clarke was the midwife for what became a burgeoning incentive travel industry in Hawai'i. For eleven years, she built her business on Maui, innovating and establishing best practices in the incentive, meetings and group travel business as she helped the industry grow. In 1988, she expanded her business to all islands and moved to Hawai'i Island, raising seven children along the way.

Originally labeled a "ground handler," the Hawai'i Visitors Bureau reclassified her profession as a Destination Management Company (DMC) in the mid-eighties. "Impossible" was not a word in Clarke's vocabulary and every challenge was an opportunity. She pioneered new tours, developed unique venues and created exciting events, enhancing Hawai'i's destination allure. In business for forty-two years, Kathy Clarke Hawai'i is the longest operating DMC in the state.

kathyclarkehawaii.com

www.ingramcontent.com/pod-product-compliance
Lightning Source LLC
Chambersburg PA
CBHW072041110526
44592CB00012B/1516